Lady Gaga

Lady Gaga

Jasper Ravenwood

CONTENTS

Introduction to Lady Gaga

Perhaps the artist most associated with the rise of international fame and the power of social media is Stefani Joanne Angelina Germanotta, better known as Lady Gaga. This cultural icon may be the preeminent representative of the twenty-first century phenomenon of outrageously famous and wealthy pop "stars". These musicians and vocalists are internationally recognized in every age cohort for more than just their music. Their lives, appearances, personalities, comments, and online posts are relentlessly devoured by the public across the globe.

Lady Gaga has managed to captivate audiences worldwide with her unique blend of musical talent, theatrical performance, and unerring dedication to her craft. Her music, which spans genres from pop and dance to jazz and rock, is complemented by her persona that often blurs the lines between reality and performance art. Stefani Germanotta's rise to fame as Lady Gaga is a story of relentless determination, reinvention, and resilience.

The main asset of an artist like Stefani Germanotta is her brand. It is a brand constantly changing to keep pace with the market, but it is also a character critically defined by what she brings to it. This brand encompasses not just her music, but her fashion, her public statements, and her activism. Has Stefani Germanotta's brand as Lady Gaga subsumed herself or has her underlying self eluded her brand? How is this self marked as uniquely abled and gendered?

Chapters of this book address the interlocking, circulatory systems of brand culture, media pressure, aesthetic genius, biography, and self-made individualism. We must delve into these elements to account for what is distinctly of this century about Lady Gaga, both as she's known by that name and as a musician with a life, a biography, an appearance, a brand, a personality, and an immense talent.

Early Life and Background

In 1986, Stefani Joanne Angelina Germanotta was born in New York City into an Italian Catholic family. Known as Lady Gaga, she studied music at an early age and created her first piano ballad when she was only 13 years old. Throughout her early teenage years, Gaga had been performing at open mic nights and acting in school plays, and by age 14, she began composing music.

Her upbringing in a close-knit Italian family instilled in her a strong work ethic and a sense of resilience. Stefani's parents, Cynthia and Joseph Germanotta, supported her artistic endeavors from a young age, enrolling her in music lessons and encouraging her to pursue her passion for performance. Her father, an internet entrepreneur, and her mother, a business executive, provided her with a stable and supportive environment that allowed her creativity to flourish.

At 17, she was able to join a musical theater company by invitation and gained early admission to the Lee Strasberg Theatre Institute. This prestigious institution was renowned for its method acting training, and it provided Gaga with the foundation she needed to hone her performance skills. However, she did not complete her degree, choosing instead to pursue her burgeoning music career full-time. Soon, at the age of 19, she was signed by Def Jam Recordings but was dropped by the company only after three months.

Following her early attempts to get her voice heard, Gaga's persistence and endurance paid off when she caught the eye of singer Akon in 2007. Akon quickly signed her to his own label, Kon Live Distribution, making Lady Gaga both the first and only recording artist on the label. Identifying her talent early on, Akon noted in an interview that he was drawn to her audacity and determination, molding her into a new persona with a refined name. This gamble in rebranding Stefani Germanotta as a pop sensation was the beginning of Lady Gaga's rise to stardom.

Rise to Fame in the Music Industry

In March 2015, Lady Gaga appeared on the cover of The New York Times Magazine with a display of face paint as her most noticeable feature. The editors of the weekly publication explained their choice of cover in the article title: "Why Lady Gaga's Outrageous Stunts Still Work." This essay will examine how her image has influenced her career trajectory. Efforts will be made to critically examine why the pop superstar has attracted little attention from academic scholarship thus far.

Just over a decade ago, Lady Gaga's songs could be heard on commercial radio in North America with the same frequency that they were being played in the European clubs. Songs like 'Just Dance' and 'Poker Face' were not only commercially popular; they were also critically acclaimed. The year 2009 saw the singer and songwriter reach the No. 50 spot on the Billboard Year End Hot 100. This is particularly impressive because she managed to accomplish this without becoming a permanent resident of the United States or growing up in record industry hub cities like Atlanta or New York City.

According to a biography in Celebrity Profile, Lady Gaga was determined to work in the music industry and her parents' wealth did not play a role in providing her with the opportunities to record her first single CD "Just Dance." The first part of the chapter focuses solely on Stefani Germanotta's training, aspirations, and troubles with her initial record deals. It details how she formed the End Records label, was signed to Def Jam Recordings, and was eventually dropped from the label after ninety days there. Just two days after losing her

Just two days after losing her big-name deal, RedOne contacted her to record two singles for the Pussycat Dolls. RedOne later contacted her again to work with the producer and recording artist Akon. A deal was struck with Akon, leading to the release of her debut album in 2008. This album marked the beginning of Lady Gaga's meteoric rise to fame.

Lady Gaga's breakthrough came with the release of her debut single "Just Dance" in 2008, which became an instant hit, topping charts worldwide. This success was quickly followed by her second single, "Poker Face," which solidified her status as a pop icon. Her debut album, "The Fame," released later that year, was both a commercial and critical success, earning her multiple awards and nominations.

Lady Gaga's unique style and persona quickly set her apart from other artists. Her elaborate costumes, theatrical performances, and avant-garde fashion choices became her trademarks. She was not just a singer; she was a performer who brought a new level of artistry and creativity to the pop music scene. Her performances were often described as "out of this world," and she became known for her ability to push the boundaries of what was considered acceptable in mainstream pop culture.

By 2009, Lady Gaga's star was firmly on the rise. Her follow-up EP, "The Fame Monster," continued her success with hits like "Bad Romance," "Telephone," and "Alejandro." She embarked on her first headlining tour, "The Monster Ball Tour," which became one of the highest-grossing tours of all time. Her ability to connect with her audience through her music and performances made her a global phenomenon.

Expanded Content: Lady Gaga's Artistic Evolution and Impact

Lady Gaga's evolution as an artist has been marked by her constant reinvention and willingness to take risks. She has never been content to rest on her laurels and is always looking for ways to push herself creatively. This drive has led her to explore various musical genres, from pop and dance to jazz and rock.

In 2011, she released her second studio album, "Born This Way," which continued to build on her success. The album's title track became an anthem for the LGBTQ+ community, promoting self-acceptance and empowerment. The album also saw Gaga exploring more mature themes and experimenting with new sounds. Tracks like "Judas" and "Marry the Night" showcased her versatility as an artist and her ability to blend different musical styles seamlessly.

Gaga's influence extended beyond her music. She became a fashion icon, known for her daring and often controversial outfits. Her collaboration with designer Alexander McQueen, in particular, produced some of her most memorable looks. She also used her platform to advocate for various social causes, including LGBTQ+ rights, mental health awareness, and anti-bullying efforts. Her Born This Way Foundation, established in 2012, has been instrumental in promoting kindness, bravery, and mental health among young people.

In 2013, Lady Gaga released her third studio album, "Artpop," which saw her returning to her dance-pop roots while incorporating elements of electronic and experimental music. The album's lead single, "Applause," received positive reviews and was a commercial success. However, "Artpop" was met with mixed reviews from critics and fans, leading some to question whether Gaga had lost her creative spark. Despite this, she continued to push boundaries and explore new artistic directions.

Lady Gaga's career took another significant turn in 2014 when she collaborated with legendary jazz singer Tony Bennett on the album "Cheek to Cheek." The album, which featured jazz standards and duets, was a critical and commercial success, earning Gaga her sixth Grammy Award. This collaboration showcased her versatility as an artist and her ability to excel in different musical genres. It also introduced her to a new audience and demonstrated her commitment to her craft.

The Continued Impact of Lady Gaga

Lady Gaga's impact on popular culture cannot be overstated. She has consistently pushed the boundaries of what is possible in music, fashion, and performance art. Her ability to reinvent herself and remain relevant in an ever-changing industry is a testament to her talent and determination.

In 2016, Gaga released her fifth studio album, "Joanne," which saw her embracing a more stripped-down, country-inspired sound. The album was a departure from her previous work but was well-received by critics and fans alike. The lead single, "Million Reasons," became a hit and showcased Gaga's powerful vocals and emotional depth.

Gaga's versatility as an artist was further demonstrated in 2018 with the release of the film "A Star is Born," in which she starred opposite Bradley Cooper. Her performance was critically acclaimed, earning her an Academy Award for Best Original Song for "Shallow," as well as nominations for Best Actress. This success cemented her status as a multi-talented artist capable of excelling in both music and acting.

In 2020, Lady Gaga returned to her dance-pop roots with the release of her sixth studio album, "Chromatica." The album received positive reviews and was a commercial success, with singles like "Stupid Love" and "Rain on Me" (featuring Ariana Grande) topping the charts. "Chromatica" showcased Gaga's ability to adapt to current musical trends while maintaining her unique style and artistry.

Conclusion

Lady Gaga's journey from Stefani Joanne Angelina Germanotta to a global pop icon is a story of perseverance, creativity, and reinvention. Her ability to continually evolve as an artist and remain at the forefront of popular culture is a testament to her talent and drive. As Lady Gaga continues to shape the music industry and influence future generations of artists, her legacy as one of the most influential pop stars of the twenty-first century is firmly cemented.

1

Lady Gaga's Musical Style and Influences

Lady Gaga's musical style and influences are a vibrant tapestry woven from the threads of multiple genres, eras, and iconic artists. Her ability to blend these elements into a unique and compelling sound has made her one of the most innovative figures in contemporary pop music.

Some are hesitant to pay serious attention to the cultural and artistic relevance of Stefani Germanotta's popular music persona, Lady Gaga; others would argue that her contribution far outpaces the attention she has been given. The assertion that Lady Gaga's music represents a creative and significant contribution to popular music culture is one that has existed for over a decade. To approach a full understanding of her art is to consider all possible angles.

One of the most striking characteristics of Lady Gaga's music is her open invitation for interpretation. Almost exclusively, her music sits at the intersection of Electro-Disco Dance and Pop, with performances often revealing an older, acoustic, stripped-back sound. Thus, following popular media criticism and sentiment, Lady Gaga might even be called an inclusivist, in terms of context, historically speaking. It is the view of several music scholars and critics that she is part of the pop idiosyncrasy avant-garde and that her music challenges all previous notions of what Pop is and what it is supposed to sound and/or look like.

Diverse Influences

The influences and creative antecedents that Gaga has personally mentioned in interviews and that various scholarly analyses assure can be seen in her concerts, albums, and fashion come from a wide variety of genres:

- **Glam Rock and Classic Rock**: Artists like David Bowie, Queen, and Led Zeppelin have heavily influenced Gaga's theatrical performance style and flamboyant fashion.
- **Pop Icons**: The impact of Madonna, Michael Jackson, and Prince is evident in her music videos, stage presence, and reinvention.
- **Jazz and Standards**: Her collaboration with Tony Bennett on the "Cheek to Cheek" album showcased her versatility and appreciation for classic American standards.
- **Modern Influences**: Contemporary artists like Beyoncé and Santigold also contribute to her eclectic style, blending modern pop sensibilities with her unique twist.

Evolution of Musical Style

Lady Gaga's musical journey is characterized by constant evolution and experimentation. Her debut album, "The Fame," introduced her as a pop and dance artist with catchy hooks and a futuristic aesthetic. Songs like "Just Dance" and "Poker Face" set the tone for her early success, combining electro-pop beats with sing-along choruses.

With "Born This Way," Gaga ventured into deeper lyrical content and more diverse musical styles. The title track became an anthem for self-acceptance, while songs like "Judas" and "Edge of Glory" explored themes of love, betrayal, and resilience, blending rock, electronic, and pop elements.

Pushing Boundaries

Gaga's willingness to push boundaries is a hallmark of her career. Her third studio album, "Artpop," exemplified this with its fusion of electronic dance music, experimental sounds, and bold visual concepts.

Despite mixed critical reception, the album showcased her ambition to innovate and challenge the status quo.

The collaboration with Tony Bennett on "Cheek to Cheek" highlighted her ability to seamlessly transition between genres. The album's success reinforced her status as a versatile artist capable of mastering jazz standards with the same prowess as pop anthems.

A Cultural Icon

Lady Gaga's impact extends beyond music. Her fashion choices, often avant-garde and boundary-pushing, have made her a fashion icon. Collaborations with designers like Alexander McQueen and Giorgio Armani have resulted in some of her most memorable looks, blending art with fashion in a way that few other artists have achieved.

Her activism, particularly in advocating for LGBTQ+ rights and mental health awareness, further solidifies her influence. The Born This Way Foundation, which she founded, continues to support and empower young people, promoting a message of kindness and bravery.

Modern Influence and Legacy

Lady Gaga's work continues to influence modern pop culture and music. Her album "Chromatica," released in 2020, marked a return to her dance-pop roots while addressing themes of healing and resilience. Tracks like "Stupid Love" and "Rain on Me" (with Ariana Grande) topped charts and resonated with fans worldwide, reaffirming her relevance in the ever-evolving music industry.

Her ability to adapt and remain innovative while staying true to her artistic vision is a key aspect of her legacy. Lady Gaga's career is a testament to the power of creativity, perseverance, and the courage to challenge conventions. As she continues to shape and inspire the music industry, her influence will undoubtedly be felt for generations to come.

2

Fashion and Visual Aesthetics: The Evolution of La

Lady Gaga's visual aesthetic is an integral part of her artistry, serving as a powerful means of self-expression and storytelling. Her fashion choices have continually pushed boundaries, challenging societal norms and redefining the role of fashion in pop culture.

BoF, a leading e-zine on fashion and culture, remarked that Gaga dances herself clean while dressed in a bespoke white Joanne Hynes one-piece, complete with green satin ruffle detailing. Her prismatic glasses are by Zambesi designers Dayne Johnston and Liz Findlay, while her Michael Jackson-esque socks are kite socks by Japanese designer Pouend Aoi. All of this proves the potential of high-fashion aesthetics, visual storytelling, and individual identity. For Lady Gaga, these dimensions constructed a body of work inviting of study and critical appreciation.

As fashion serves by reflecting the self, Lady Gaga's Family Portrait—performances, album art, media interviews, and other mediums of self-expression—showcases an apparatus of her subjectivity. It is a carefully wrought demonstration of the limitless qualities of humanity, society, and the art world.

Early Influence and the Birth of an Icon

In the early days of album development, Lady Gaga was zombified by the industry and went through a dark period of automatic writing that turned out the frenzied Fame. The public quickly noticed her and was deeply fascinated by her Bonapartean utility in molding celebrity image through a variety of outlets. As Gaga comes into her own as a celebrity figure, the cult of celebrity will never be the same again. As high concept becomes everything, visual change becomes everything, as the negatives mutate before us to become a compelling revelation of the self.

The Fusion of Art and Fashion

Tracing a broader social phenomenon of the '80s in which art as spectacle was merged with thematic self-creations, Gaga utilizes pop knowledge to redefine the celebrity trope within contemporary youth culture. Her fashion choices often serve as a commentary on fame, identity, and society's obsession with celebrity. Gaga's partnership with designers like Alexander McQueen, Donatella Versace, and Giorgio Armani has led to some of her most iconic looks, from the infamous meat dress to her alienesque appearances at award shows.

Each outfit, meticulously crafted and often theatrical, tells a story. Her meat dress, for example, worn to the 2010 MTV Video Music Awards, sparked conversations about feminism, body autonomy, and animal rights. This avant-garde approach to fashion is not just about shock value; it's a calculated effort to challenge perceptions and provoke thought.

Redefining Gender and Identity

Lady Gaga's fashion also plays a crucial role in her exploration of gender and identity. She often blends masculine and feminine elements, creating a fluid representation of self. This approach aligns with her advocacy for LGBTQ+ rights and her message of self-acceptance. Outfits that blur the lines between gender norms, such as her tuxedo-inspired ensembles and exaggerated makeup, serve to empower her fans and promote inclusivity.

Evolution through Albums

With each album, Gaga's visual style evolves to reflect her musical journey. "The Fame" and "The Fame Monster" eras were characterized by futuristic and bold looks that mirrored her electronic dance-pop sound. The "Born This Way" era saw her embracing a more raw and edgy aesthetic, aligning with the album's themes of self-acceptance and empowerment.

"Artpop" brought a kaleidoscope of colors and abstract designs, emphasizing the album's experimental nature. Her collaboration with Tony Bennett on "Cheek to Cheek" showcased a more classic and refined elegance, reflecting the jazz standards they performed together. "Joanne" marked a significant shift to a more stripped-back, country-inspired look, symbolizing a return to her roots and a more personal, introspective phase.

The Power of Visual Storytelling

Lady Gaga's visual storytelling extends beyond her fashion choices. Her music videos, performances, and public appearances are carefully crafted to convey specific messages and themes. Videos like "Bad Romance" and "Telephone" are mini cinematic experiences that combine music, fashion, and narrative to create a lasting impact.

Her Super Bowl halftime performance in 2017 is a prime example of how she uses visual elements to enhance her music. The performance was a spectacle of lights, costumes, and choreography, all working together to create a powerful statement of unity and resilience.

Legacy and Influence

Lady Gaga's influence on fashion and visual aesthetics is undeniable. She has inspired countless artists and designers, pushing them to think outside the box and embrace their creativity. Her ability to continually reinvent herself while maintaining her unique identity is a testament to her artistry and vision.

As fashion serves by reflecting the self, Lady Gaga's body of work—performances, album art, media interviews, and other mediums of self-expression—showcases an apparatus of her subjectivity. It is a carefully wrought demonstration of the limitless qualities of humanity, society, and the art world. Her contributions to fashion and visual aesthetics have not only redefined the celebrity trope but have also opened up new possibilities for artistic expression in contemporary youth culture.

Activism and Social Justice Work

Lady Gaga's public persona may incite controversy and place her firmly in the "pop star" space, yet she much more accurately embodies the role of a public figure, using her platform to elicit social change and draw attention to worthwhile causes and organizations. Her dedication to activism and social justice is a central aspect of her career and personal identity.

In 2012, the Harvard University Foundation awarded her the Peter J. Gomes Humanitarian Award in honor of her commitment to promoting equality and her activist work. This recognition was a testament to her efforts in using her fame for philanthropic endeavors and social advocacy.

Born This Way Foundation

Lady Gaga announced the creation of the Born This Way Foundation in late 2011, along with her mother, Cynthia Germanotta. Born This Way focuses on youth empowerment and addresses issues such as self-confidence, well-being, anti-bullying, mentoring, career development, and advocacy. The foundation aims to create a kinder and braver world by supporting the wellness of young people and empowering them to create positive change in their communities. It is now known as the Born This Way Fund in America.

The foundation's initiatives include mental health resources, leadership programs, and partnerships with other organizations to amplify its impact. Lady Gaga's personal experiences with bullying and mental health struggles have informed the foundation's mission, making it a deeply personal project for her.

Mayor of Los Angeles (Honorary)

In November 2019, the City of Los Angeles announced that Lady Gaga was to be LA's newest "mayor." This honorary and cheeky title was bestowed on her as a caretaker position. It recognized her as a resident filmmaker, songwriter, troublemaker, and activist responsible for significant cultural shifts and critical examination of the music industry and its spheres of influence.

This honor reflected her impact on the city's cultural landscape and her efforts to use her art and influence to drive positive change. It highlighted her role as a catalyst for social movements and her ability to inspire others through her work.

Advocacy for the LGBTQ+ Community

Throughout the years, Lady Gaga has played a large role in social and advocacy movements, particularly in support of the LGBTQ+ community. Her pieces contain powerful messages related to equality, politics, and empowerment. Her song "Born This Way" became an anthem for the LGBTQ+ community, promoting self-acceptance and celebrating diversity. She has used her platform to advocate for LGBTQ+ rights, speaking out against discrimination and supporting marriage equality.

Lady Gaga's performances and public appearances often include references to LGBTQ+ issues, further emphasizing her commitment to the cause. She has been a vocal advocate for policies that protect LGBTQ+ individuals and has used her influence to support organizations that provide resources and support to the community.

Messages of Equality and Empowerment

A recurring theme in Lady Gaga's solo work is the need for self-confidence and self-expression. She encourages her fans to embrace their individuality and stand up against bullying and discrimination. Her music often explores themes of self-acceptance, resilience, and personal freedom, resonating with audiences who feel marginalized or misunderstood.

In addition to her work with the Born This Way Foundation, Lady Gaga has supported various causes through fundraising efforts and public advocacy. She has raised awareness about mental health, HIV/AIDS, and women's rights, using her platform to amplify the voices of those who are often overlooked.

Racial Justice and "Chromatica"

Racial justice was added to her musical pursuits with her alter ego on the album "Chromatica." The album's themes of healing and resilience are complemented by Gaga's advocacy for racial equality and social justice. Through her music and public statements, she has shown solidarity with movements like Black Lives Matter and has called for systemic change to address racial injustice.

Lady Gaga's activism is not limited to her music; it permeates every aspect of her public life. She continues to use her influence to challenge the status quo and advocate for a more inclusive and equitable world. Her commitment to social justice and her ability to inspire change make her a powerful force in both the music industry and the broader cultural landscape.

Lady Gaga in Film and Television

Lady Gaga is not just a pop superstar but also an accomplished actress, featuring in both film and television. She has taken on comedic and dramatic roles, at times portraying altered versions of her pop persona. Furthermore, she has produced documentary films about herself to claim ownership over her image. Across these various media, Lady Gaga has reached peak celebrity status and sustained her position as a leading figure in pop culture. She has ultimately achieved this status by consistently challenging stereotypes about what it means to exist as a movie star, prominent network actor, and high-grossing singer.

Lady Gaga's Acting Career

Lady Gaga's acting career is a seamless blend of her musical talents and the "live" nature of her persona. Her ability to perform and embody various characters has allowed her to transition smoothly from the stage to the screen. In fact, she was signed to be the lead character in the "A Star Is Born" remake because of her vocal talents and her clear capacity to perform in a musical setting. When she is in the process of creating work for her Little Monsters, who are quickly becoming her little stars, she is at her best. Simultaneity functions as an important quality within the work Lady Gaga creates.

"A Star Is Born"

"A Star Is Born" (2018) was a significant milestone in Lady Gaga's acting career. Directed by Bradley Cooper, the film tells the story of a seasoned musician who discovers and falls in love with a struggling artist. Lady Gaga's portrayal of Ally, the lead character, earned her critical acclaim and showcased her ability to deliver powerful performances both musically and dramatically. Her performance in the film was praised for its authenticity and emotional depth, earning her an Academy Award nomination for Best Actress and winning the Oscar for Best Original Song with "Shallow."

American Horror Story

Her latest career move as an actress in "American Horror Story" is a testament to her fulfillment of postcinema's goals and values. Not only does Lady Gaga strive to use contested forms of media to advance her own career, but she also aims to prove that televisual acting, as an act of participation in 'new' forms of storytelling (i.e., postcinematic content), is as inextricable from the ongoing validation of her brand as pop music. In "American Horror Story: Hotel" (2015-2016), Gaga took on the role of The Countess, a glamorous and deadly vampire. Her performance won her a Golden Globe Award for Best Actress in a Limited Series or Television Film, further solidifying her status as a versatile and talented actress.

Documentary Work

Lady Gaga has also used documentary films to provide a more intimate look into her life and career. "Gaga: Five Foot Two" (2017), a Netflix documentary, offers an unfiltered glimpse into her world, showcasing her struggles with chronic pain, the making of her album "Joanne," and her preparations for the Super Bowl halftime show. This documentary allowed her to claim ownership over her image and narrative, providing fans with an authentic and raw portrayal of her life.

Future Projects and Legacy

Lady Gaga continues to expand her acting portfolio with upcoming roles and projects. Her ability to seamlessly transition between music, film, and television underscores her versatility as an artist. She has proven that she is not confined to a single medium and can excel in various forms of entertainment.

Her commitment to challenging stereotypes and pushing boundaries has made her a trailblazer in the entertainment industry. Lady

Gaga's influence extends beyond her music, as she continues to redefine what it means to be a multi-faceted artist in today's media landscape.

Impact on LGBTQ+ Community

Lady Gaga's legacy boasts a variety of substantial achievements, but her meaningful and multifaceted relationship with the LGBTQ+ community is considered one of her most impactful feats. Her advocacy for LGBTQ+ rights and her dedication to promoting equality have earned her a place among the most influential allies of the community.

Empowerment Anthem: "Born This Way"

In 2011, Lady Gaga penned the LGBTQ+-friendly empowerment anthem "Born This Way." This song became a cultural phenomenon, resonating with millions of people worldwide. Released on February 11, 2011, the track spent six weeks at the top of the Billboard Hot Dance Club Songs chart and has sold over 10 million units. More than its chart statistics, "Born This Way" has left a lasting mark on the LGBTQ+ community. The song's message of self-acceptance and celebration of diversity has inspired countless individuals to embrace their true selves and stand up against discrimination.

Advocacy and Activism

The activists and allies behind Lady Gaga's record label, lawyers, and partners represent roughly 27 leading organizations in the field of LGBTQ+ rights. Her activism extends beyond music and into her public and personal life. In 2015, after visiting the White House and advocating for the eradication of dangerous and debunked conversion therapy practices, she delivered a powerful speech in Portland just days before the Pulse nightclub massacre. This tragic event further galvanized her commitment to the cause.

Lady Gaga's efforts to support the LGBTQ+ community also include writing an op-ed for Billboard, where she addressed critical issues facing the community and called for action. Her engagement with political and social movements demonstrates her dedication to using her platform for positive change.

Influence and Legacy

Within the storied pantheon of LGBTQ allydom, which includes the likes of Barbra Streisand, Madonna, Elton John, and Cher, Lady Gaga's contributions account for a sizeable chunk of her rapidly accumulating biography. Her influence extends beyond her music, as she continually advocates for the rights and well-being of LGBTQ+ individuals.

Personal Connection and Cultural Impact

For lesbian, gay, and bisexual individuals in the United States who have experienced marginalization and prejudice, "Born This Way" has been a catalyst for positive social change. It has helped to galvanize one of the most quickly growing civil rights movements of our generation. Lady Gaga's Italian-American Catholic background adds another layer of intrigue to her work, as she challenges traditional norms and expectations.

Her ability to break down barriers within the pop industrial complex and to use her platform to advocate for social justice has cemented her place as a powerful force for change. Lady Gaga's ongoing efforts to support the LGBTQ+ community continue to inspire and empower individuals around the world.

Lady Gaga's Global Fanbase

There are a number of other stars with large and passionate fandoms. However, none of these fandoms come close to having the global reach of the Lady Gaga fanbase. Lady Gaga's fans, affectionately known as "Little Monsters," fellowship in over twenty different forums across the five inhabited continents. The unwavering dedication and diverse backgrounds of her fans have cemented her as a truly global phenomenon.

Diversity and Reach of the Fanbase

Lady Gaga attracts a significant number of American fans, including English-speaking fans in the United States, Canada, Australia, and Great Britain. Additionally, she has garnered a substantial following among foreign-born residents of these countries who find it easier to communicate with their fellow Little Monsters in English. This wide-reaching appeal is further evidenced by the immense popularity of her YouTube videos and social media presence in various regions around the world.

Popularity in Asia

Slevin pointed to the immense popularity of her YouTube videos in South Korea and Thailand, as well as high online rankings in these countries. Her unique style and inclusive message resonate strongly with fans in these regions, contributing to a robust online community that actively engages with her content.

European Fanbase

Afanasiev drew attention to her fans in Eastern Europe, particularly in Russia, Ukraine, and Poland. Despite cultural and language differences, these fans have embraced Lady Gaga's music and persona, creating vibrant communities that share concert dates, videos, and news updates. White also highlights how Greek fans have embraced Lady Gaga despite initial reservations about American superstars, illustrating her ability to transcend cultural barriers.

Middle Eastern and Latin American Following

Erdem cited blog posts by one of the handful of Turkish interviews translated from Turkish-language news articles in several blogs. This indicates a growing interest and appreciation for Lady Gaga in the Middle East, where fans connect over shared translations and discussions of her work.

Vargas highlighted that a 40-season, continent-wide general audience entertainment magazine and website in Latin America covered Lady Gaga's visit to Brazil extensively. This coverage underscores her popularity in Latin America, where fans eagerly follow her career and celebrate her visits to their countries.

Japanese Fan Culture

Meanwhile, Mauner mentioned Gaga when describing a trip to Tokyo, providing numerous accounts of Japanese fans. These fans, referred to by Mauner as "NIPPONSTER for all the fans outside of Japan," demonstrate the depth of her influence in Japan. Little Monsters in at least 18 countries worldwide regularly communicate on social networks, posting concert tour dates, videos, recordings, reviews, and news to each other.

Multilingual Engagement

An impressive testament to her global impact is the translation of her song lyrics into multiple languages. There are 77 non-English translations of Lady Gaga's songs online, compared to just five translations of TI's "Paper Trail" and fifteen translations of Beatles' tracks. This suggests that fans, rather than the pop star herself, often initiate the translation of her lyrics. The emotional resonance of her music inspires fans to share it with others in their native languages, further extending her reach.

Emotional Connection

Lady Gaga's ability to connect with her fans on an emotional level is a significant factor in her widespread popularity. Her messages of self-acceptance, empowerment, and individuality resonate deeply with people from diverse backgrounds. This connection fosters a sense of community among her fans, who support one another and share their experiences through online forums and social media.

Conclusion

The global reach of Lady Gaga's fanbase is unparalleled, reflecting the universal appeal of her music, message, and persona. Her ability to inspire and connect with fans from all corners of the globe underscores her influence as a cultural icon. Little Monsters, united by their admiration for Lady Gaga, continue to celebrate her work and contribute to her enduring legacy as one of the most beloved and influential pop stars of our time.

7

Collaborations and Duets with Other Artists

The discussion of Stefani Germanotta's success would be incomplete without mentioning Lady Gaga's collaborative efforts with other artists. From the very beginning of her solo career, Lady Gaga has performed duets and collaborated with a diverse array of musicians, enhancing her music's reach and depth.

Early Collaborations

One of Lady Gaga's earliest collaborations was with the British synthpop band Pet Shop Boys on the composition and video of "3-Way." This early venture into collaborative work set the stage for future partnerships. Her openness to working with other artists became evident almost immediately after the release of her debut album, "The Fame."

Partnership with Tony Bennett

A notable and lengthy collaboration began with jazz legend Tony Bennett. As early as 2011, during their joint performance at the Grammy Awards, the two-generation gap between them was bridged by their shared love for jazz. Their chemistry led to the creation of the Grammy-winning album "Cheek to Cheek" in 2014, featuring a collection of jazz standards. This partnership showcased Gaga's versatility and highlighted her ability to seamlessly transition between different musical genres.

Diverse Collaborations

Lady Gaga's discography over the years includes a mix of solo and duo tracks that display the diversity of her inspirations and interests. Her willingness to experiment with different styles is evident in her wide-ranging collaborations:

- **Colby O'Donis**: Gaga's early work with rapper Colby O'Donis on "Just Dance" helped catapult her into the mainstream.
- **Beyoncé**: The powerful collaboration on the song "Telephone" became an iconic pop anthem, merging their unique styles and fanbases.
- **Christina Aguilera**: Their performance of "Do What U Want" on "The Voice" highlighted Gaga's ability to harmonize and connect with other powerhouse vocalists.
- **Elton John**: Gaga has performed multiple times with Elton John, including duets on "Sine from Above" from her album "Chromatica" and special performances at events.

Impact on Music Industry

These collaborations not only expanded her musical repertoire but also brought new dimensions to her artistry. Working with artists from different genres allowed Lady Gaga to explore various musical landscapes, from electronic and disco sounds to big-band swing and torch songs. Her ability to adapt and excel in diverse musical environments has cemented her status as a versatile and innovative artist.

Collaborative Albums and Projects

Gaga's collaborative spirit extends beyond single tracks. Her joint album with Tony Bennett, "Cheek to Cheek," and its follow-up "Love for Sale" (2021), which also won a Grammy, demonstrate her commitment to deep, meaningful partnerships in music. These projects required extensive studio time and dedication, reflecting her passion for creating authentic and high-quality music.

Legacy of Collaborations

Lady Gaga's collaborations have contributed to her lasting legacy in the music industry. Her ability to form successful partnerships and create memorable music with a variety of artists showcases her adaptability and broad appeal. The renaissance of extended song duets, brought about by such collaborative efforts, continues to influence contemporary music.

Conclusion

Lady Gaga's collaborative efforts have played a significant role in her career, allowing her to explore different musical genres and connect with a wide range of artists. From early collaborations to her ongoing partnership with Tony Bennett, Gaga's duets and joint projects highlight her versatility and commitment to artistic excellence. These collaborations have enriched her musical journey and solidified her position as a pioneering and influential figure in the music industry.

8

Awards and Achievements

Lady Gaga's body of work has been recognized with numerous awards and accolades across music, film, fashion, and philanthropy. Her impact spans various realms, making her a multifaceted icon celebrated worldwide.

Music and Film Awards

Lady Gaga's contributions to music and film have earned her numerous prestigious awards. She has received multiple Grammy Awards, recognizing her exceptional talent and innovation in the music industry. Her groundbreaking albums like "The Fame," "Born This Way," and "Chromatica" have been celebrated for their creative brilliance and cultural impact.

In the film industry, Lady Gaga's performance in "A Star Is Born" garnered critical acclaim, earning her an Academy Award for Best Original Song for "Shallow." Her portrayal of Ally in the film also earned her a nomination for Best Actress, further cementing her status as a versatile and talented performer.

Fashion and Visual Impact

Lady Gaga's stylistic choices have transcended the realm of pop music, influencing the worlds of art and fashion. Her album covers and iconic outfits have been replicated by drag queens and celebrated in fashion circles. A waxwork statue of Lady Gaga can be viewed in various Madame Tussauds around the world, a testament to her enduring influence.

Retail partnerships featuring Lady Gaga's fashion choices have seen increased publicity for these brands, thanks to her one-of-a-kind red carpet appearances. Her fashion legacy continues to inspire designers and fashion enthusiasts globally.

Philanthropic Efforts

In the realm of charity, Lady Gaga has been instrumental in fostering an inclusive and supportive environment. She has successfully rallied other celebrities to volunteer their time and resources for various causes, including mental health awareness, COVID-19 relief efforts, and scholarships for communities facing discrimination. Her charitable endeavors have gained widespread attention, both in charity news outlets and across social media.

Humanitarian Recognitions

Lady Gaga has received numerous honors from her native New York and the U.S. more broadly. In 2011, she was awarded the UNICEF Danny Kaye Humanitarian Award for her work with the organization's projects on behalf of children. Acceptance speeches by stars including Patti Lupone and Bette Midler highlighted Lady Gaga as a symbol of New York ambition and inclusion.

She also received the key to West Hollywood for her support of unions, reflecting her commitment to social justice and community advocacy. Additionally, a ribbon-cutting ceremony for the SMAAC charter school in 2011 featured Lady Gaga's music and a stage dedicated in her name.

Partnerships and Collaborations

A Lady Gaga partnership with Virgin Mobile has helped ensure that mental health is seen as a community issue as well as an individual concern. The Times Square launch of the Born This Way phone, underwritten by Virgin Mobile, included 20 performances of "Gaga by Gaga," an off-Broadway play produced by the mental health charity Creative Alternatives of New York.

Conclusion

Lady Gaga's awards and achievements reflect her remarkable talent, creativity, and commitment to making a positive impact in various fields. From music and film to fashion and philanthropy, her influence continues to grow, inspiring countless individuals around the world. Her legacy as an artist and humanitarian is a testament to her dedication to excellence and her unwavering support for those in need.

9

Lady Gaga's Entrepreneurial Ventures

In keeping with her carefully cultivated multifaceted and entrepreneurial public persona, Lady Gaga has created a number of ventures off stage, extending her portfolio to include clothing, cosmetics, and technology. Her business acumen and creativity have led to the development of successful enterprises that reflect her unique style and values.

Haus Labs

One of Lady Gaga's most prominent ventures is Haus Labs, an online store she founded in 2019. The brand focuses on vegan cosmetics, particularly eye makeup, and aims to promote self-expression and inclusivity. Haus Labs offers a wide range of products, bundled in various ways including collections, kits, duos, trios, and quads. The brand's commitment to cruelty-free and vegan ingredients aligns with Gaga's advocacy for ethical consumerism and environmental sustainability. The brand's motto, "Our Haus, Your Rules," encapsulates Gaga's vision of empowering individuals to explore their identities through makeup.

Ate My Heart

In 2016, Lady Gaga incorporated Ate My Heart, a company that sells clothing, decorative art, and fashion accessories. The company takes its name from a line in her 2008 song "Love Game." Ate My Heart's first official line, the Joanne Trattoria Collection, was inspired and created with Lady Gaga's parents. Although she left the business nine months after its formation and retained no financial stake, the designs were marketed and distributed on her e-commerce site and at the Joanne Trattoria Restaurant, which is run by her father. The collection featured unique pieces that blended Gaga's distinctive style with her family's heritage, creating a personal and heartfelt brand.

Culinary Ventures

In 2012, Lady Gaga and her personal chef began working together to create recipes for "Born This Way"-inspired family meals. These meals not only bear her name but also share the album's messages of mental health awareness and acceptance. Plans exist to expand and sell these and other recipes through a chain of restaurants co-branded with her parents under the name "Love Bravery at Joanne Trattoria." These culinary ventures reflect Gaga's commitment to promoting mental health and well-being through nourishing, comforting food.

Philanthropic Foundations

Prior to releasing her album in 2013, Lady Gaga created a foundation to grant scholarships and work toward youth empowerment. The foundation addresses issues such as self-confidence, well-being, anti-bullying, mentoring, and career development. Her philanthropic efforts are aimed at creating a kinder, more inclusive world, reflecting the messages of empowerment and acceptance that permeate her music.

Encouraging Female Entrepreneurs

At the 2018 Billboard Women in Music event in New York, Lady Gaga recommended that aspiring female entrepreneurs consider careers as businesswomen. She has been an advocate for women in business, encouraging them to pursue their entrepreneurial dreams. During a makeup summit in 2019, she introduced a contest to fund and support new Lady Gaga beauty entrepreneurs, further demonstrating her commitment to nurturing and empowering the next generation of businesswomen.

Future Ventures

Lady Gaga's entrepreneurial spirit continues to drive her to explore new ventures. It has been announced that she and her business partners

Vesel Youth and Ikonomakidduxof are producing the Kennedy Holistic Beauty Center. This center will be part of a new commerce complex opposite New York's Central Park, aiming to integrate wellness and beauty in a holistic approach. The center will offer a range of services and products that align with Gaga's vision of promoting mental health and overall well-being.

Conclusion

Lady Gaga's entrepreneurial ventures are a testament to her creativity, business acumen, and commitment to making a positive impact. From cosmetics to clothing, from food to philanthropy, her ventures reflect her multifaceted talents and her dedication to promoting self-expression, inclusivity, and mental health awareness. Her efforts continue to inspire and empower individuals around the world, further solidifying her legacy as not just a pop icon but also a successful entrepreneur and humanitarian.

10

Lady Gaga's Personal Life and Philanthropy

Lady Gaga's personal life reveals that she is far more than a singer and performer. As Stefani Germanotta, Gaga is a daughter, a sister, and a partner who is part of a close-knit Italian-American family. Her fiancé, Taylor Kinney, has played the male lead in several of her video clips, demonstrating their strong personal and professional connection.

Lessons Learned from Her Parents

Both Joe and Cynthia Germanotta are engaged in charitable endeavors and play significant roles in Stefani's life. Here are three key lessons that Lady Gaga, affectionately known as "Mother Monster," has learned from her parents:

1. **Work Ethic and Resilience**: Stefani inherited her father's challenging yet determined sensibility. Joe Germanotta's work in the food business, which even led to his appearance on the American reality TV show "The Real Housewives of New Jersey," taught her the importance of perseverance and dedication. Despite their appearances, the Germanottas are not counted among the extremely wealthy, and Stefani's upbringing in a private Catholic all-girls school instilled a sense of hard work and humility.

2. **Chivalry and Integrity**: Her father's old-school chivalry and integrity have significantly shaped Stefani's character. These qualities have influenced her interactions and relationships, both

personally and professionally. She strives to embody the same respect and honor in her dealings with others.

3. **Nurturing Dreams and Creativity**: Cynthia Germanotta allowed her daughter to cultivate her dreams, particularly in artistic development. This nurturing environment enabled Lady Gaga to explore her creativity freely, leading to her unique and bold artistic expressions. Cynthia's support for her daughter's ambitions has been a cornerstone of Lady Gaga's success.

Balancing Private Life and Public Persona

Distinguishing Stefani Germanotta from Lady Gaga can be challenging. As Lady Gaga, she often appears to be 'on' even in her personal life. In Steplin's words, characters such as Lady Gaga "seem to be a very real part of the person playing the role, much more like a well-worn wardrobe than an easily shedding set of novelty clothes," which also applies to Stefani Germanotta. Many of her life experiences have directly informed her Lady Gaga persona, blending her private and public identities seamlessly.

Impact of Personal Experiences on Philanthropy

Many of Stefani Germanotta's most telling life experiences have directly influenced her philanthropic efforts. For example, her family experienced eviction at one point, which profoundly impacted her views on social justice. This life event ignited her drive to address issues such as fighting HIV/AIDS, advocating for safe communities, preventing bullying, and inspiring young people.

Key Philanthropic Areas

Lady Gaga's philanthropy focuses on four key areas:

1. **Fighting HIV/AIDS**: She has been actively involved in campaigns and initiatives aimed at combating HIV/AIDS, raising awareness, and supporting those affected by the disease.

2. **Advocating for Safe Communities**: Lady Gaga advocates for creating safe, inclusive communities where individuals can express themselves without fear of discrimination or violence.
3. **Preventing Bullying**: Through the Born This Way Foundation and other initiatives, she works to prevent bullying and promote kindness and acceptance, particularly among young people.
4. **Inspiring Young People**: She is dedicated to empowering youth, encouraging them to embrace their uniqueness and pursue their dreams.

Research and Public Mission

In researching Lady Gaga, evidence of a connection between her personal life and public mission becomes clear. Rather than hiding behind her public persona, Stefani Germanotta's experiences emerge as key factors driving her dedication to philanthropy and social change. This connection underscores the authenticity of her efforts and the genuine passion behind her advocacy work.

Conclusion

Lady Gaga's personal life and philanthropy reflect her depth as an individual and her commitment to making a positive impact. Her upbringing, influenced by her parents' values and support, has shaped her into a compassionate and driven leader. By addressing critical social issues and inspiring others, Lady Gaga continues to use her platform to effect meaningful change, embodying the true spirit of a modern-day philanthropist and role model.

11

Critical Reception and Controversies

In general, Lady Gaga has been unproblematically hailed as a figure of vast cultural importance. Her innovative approach to pop music has garnered critical seriousness and clout, setting her apart from other artists who have faced more negative receptions. Scholars like Inez van Sneider, Kerry Skemp, and Paloma Alonso, in their work *Diva Worship: Salvation and Resistance in the House of Gaga* (2013), highlight Gaga's demand for an androgynous modern iconography that reestablishes the full range of human potential. Similarly, Nigel Lezama, in *"Alejandro" and the Trouble with Fame and Sex as Contraband* (2014), suggests that Gaga's work transcends mere sexual themes, endorsing an ideology that insists upon the negotiability of the human in deeply provocative ways.

As an icon, Lady Gaga is invaluable for those who see her as a symbol of art, bravery, and freedom, as well as those who view her as a subversive, corrupting figure.

Significance and Problematic Biography

While Lady Gaga's significance is rarely contested, her biography is frequently problematized in line with movements away from respectability politics and toward embracing the power of the "messy feminine." Her portrayal of musical alienation, as seen in 'Just Dance's' bleak party-scene chronicling, began even before her birth. Gaga has shared that her mother's professional decision against an abortion, despite the risk posed by lupus-induced fetal seizures, was a trauma that contributed to Gaga's later struggles with dysmorphia.

Former Columbia Records talent spotter Wendell Williams has argued that questions about Gaga's originality are moot. He contends that Gaga creates scandals to preserve her public image and carve out space for artistic experimentation. This perspective sheds light on the deliberate nature of her provocative actions and public persona.

Artistic Innovation and Criticism

Lady Gaga's artistic innovation is one of the key reasons for her critical acclaim. Her ability to blend various musical genres, incorporate theatrical elements into her performances, and push the boundaries of conventional pop music has earned her a unique place in the industry. Critics have praised her for her creativity, versatility, and willingness to take risks.

However, her bold and often controversial choices have also attracted criticism. Some detractors argue that her eccentricity and shock value overshadow her musical talent. Instances like the infamous meat dress at the 2010 MTV Video Music Awards sparked debates about whether Gaga's fashion statements detracted from her artistry or enhanced her persona as a boundary-pushing artist.

Feminist Icon and Critique

Lady Gaga is often celebrated as a feminist icon for her advocacy of gender equality and empowerment. Her music and public statements frequently challenge traditional gender norms and promote self-expression. Songs like "Born This Way" and "Til It Happens to You" have been lauded for their messages of acceptance and resilience.

Yet, her feminist stance has not been without controversy. Some critics question her use of provocative imagery and performance styles, arguing that they reinforce rather than dismantle patriarchal norms. Despite these critiques, Gaga's impact on the feminist movement remains significant, as she continues to inspire conversations about gender, identity, and power dynamics in the entertainment industry.

LGBTQ+ Advocacy and Backlash

Lady Gaga's advocacy for LGBTQ+ rights has been a cornerstone of her public image. Her anthem "Born This Way" has become a rallying cry for LGBTQ+ individuals worldwide, promoting self-acceptance and pride. Gaga's activism extends beyond her music; she has been involved in numerous initiatives and organizations supporting LGBTQ+ rights.

However, her outspoken support has also faced backlash. Critics from conservative groups have accused her of promoting "immorality" and undermining traditional values. Despite this, Gaga has remained steadfast in her commitment to LGBTQ+ advocacy, using her platform to effect positive change and support marginalized communities.

Controversial Music Videos

Lady Gaga's music videos are known for their elaborate and often controversial themes. Videos like "Alejandro" and "Judas" have sparked debates about their religious and sexual imagery. "Alejandro," in particular, was criticized by some for its portrayal of religious symbols, with detractors accusing Gaga of blasphemy.

On the other hand, her fans and some critics view these videos as bold artistic statements that challenge societal norms and provoke thought. Gaga's willingness to tackle taboo subjects in her music videos has solidified her reputation as an artist unafraid to push boundaries and challenge the status quo.

Mental Health Advocacy

Lady Gaga's advocacy for mental health awareness is another aspect of her legacy that has garnered both praise and scrutiny. Through her Born This Way Foundation, she has worked to promote mental health resources, support youth empowerment, and combat bullying. Her openness about her own struggles with mental health has helped destigmatize these issues and encourage others to seek help.

Despite her positive impact, some critics argue that her celebrity status might overshadow the real issues at hand. They claim that while her efforts are commendable, the focus on her persona could detract from the broader movement to address mental health challenges. Nevertheless, Gaga's contributions to mental health advocacy continue to inspire and support many individuals around the world.

Public Image and Scandals

Lady Gaga's public image has been shaped by a series of high-profile scandals and controversies. From her provocative performances to her outspoken political views, she has often found herself at the center of media attention. These scandals, while polarizing, have also contributed to her mystique and allure as an artist who is unafraid to defy expectations.

One notable scandal involved her meat dress at the 2010 MTV Video Music Awards. The dress, made entirely of raw beef, was intended as a statement about human rights and the military's "Don't Ask, Don't Tell" policy. While some praised the boldness of the statement, others condemned it as offensive and in poor taste. Gaga's ability to generate such strong reactions speaks to her power as a provocateur and cultural figure.

Conclusion

Lady Gaga's critical reception and the controversies surrounding her highlight her multifaceted role as both a groundbreaking artist and a polarizing public figure. Her work continues to inspire and challenge societal norms, making her a subject of both adulation and critique. By embracing the complexities of her identity and pushing the boundaries of conventional pop stardom, Lady Gaga solidifies her place as a pivotal figure in contemporary culture.

Conclusion: Lady Gaga's Enduring Legacy

Inextricably linked to Lady Gaga's stature as a cultural thunderstorm is her impact on various spheres of culture and related disciplines. She has crafted an enduring legacy that touches music, fashion, activism, and art. Lady Gaga's multifaceted persona has allowed her to capture the Zeitgeist of the late twentieth and early twenty-first centuries, cementing her place as a towering cultural icon.

Unmatched Musical Talent

In the realm of music, Lady Gaga is unmatched as a singer and excels as a professional songwriter. She has penned some of the most memorable and popular songs of the past two decades. Her ability and willingness to experiment with different popular music forms—ranging from electronica, dance, country, to jazz—has afforded her a broad and diverse audience. Albums like "The Fame," "Born This Way," "Joanne," and "Chromatica" showcase her versatility and her commitment to pushing musical boundaries.

Her live performances are renowned for their theatricality and emotional depth, offering fans an immersive experience that transcends the typical concert format. Lady Gaga's powerful vocals, combined with her innovative stage designs and choreography, create an unforgettable spectacle that leaves a lasting impression on audiences worldwide.

Fashion Icon and Influence

Lady Gaga is quite literally unmatched in the fashion world. More fashion-icon than fashionista, her aesthetic, with its focus on extremes and tensional oppositions, has influenced fashion collections around the world. From her infamous meat dress to her avant-garde red carpet looks, Gaga's fashion choices have consistently challenged norms and set trends.

Her collaborations with top designers such as Alexander McQueen, Donatella Versace, and Giorgio Armani have resulted in iconic fashion moments that are celebrated and imitated globally. Gaga's ability to seamlessly blend fashion with performance art has redefined the role of a pop star, making her a muse and a trendsetter in the fashion industry.

Passionate Activism

In terms of her activism, Lady Gaga is a passionate supporter of the LGBTQ+ community, particularly the transgender community in America. Her anthem "Born This Way" has become a symbol of self-acceptance and empowerment for millions. Gaga's advocacy extends beyond music; she has actively campaigned for LGBTQ+ rights, mental health awareness, and anti-bullying initiatives through her Born This Way Foundation.

In her art and her public persona, Lady Gaga argues for and demonstrates the necessity of the political in contrast to a wider contemporary art world that often veers towards depoliticization. Her outspoken stance on social issues has inspired countless fans to become more engaged in activism and social justice.

Multifaceted Artistic Persona

The enduring response to, and legacy of, Lady Gaga, is the multifaceted artistic persona capable of capturing the spirit of the times. Continually innovating and exemplifying a commitment to fashion, music, art, and political activism that is appreciated rather than simply consumed, Lady Gaga looms over popular culture as an interminable example of the artist-as-icon.

Her predilection for multidisciplinarity and intense public presence has afforded her the kind of longevity and impact few pop musicians can claim. From her electrifying performances to her groundbreaking music videos, Lady Gaga has consistently pushed the boundaries of what it means to be a pop artist.

Cultural Impact and Legacy

As 13 years from her debut pass, and her singularity in music and pop culture comes into clearer focus, we would do well to consider Lady Gaga as a towering cultural icon—a true freak-shaped artistic anomaly. Her influence extends beyond entertainment; she has become a symbol of resilience, creativity, and unapologetic self-expression.

Lady Gaga's legacy is not only defined by her artistic achievements but also by her ability to inspire change and connect with people on a deeply personal level. Her work continues to resonate with fans across generations, ensuring that her impact will be felt for years to come.

Conclusion

Lady Gaga's enduring legacy is a testament to her unparalleled talent, creativity, and dedication to making a positive impact. Her influence in music, fashion, activism, and art transcends traditional boundaries, making her a true cultural phenomenon. As she continues to innovate and inspire, Lady Gaga's legacy as an artist, icon, and advocate will remain a vital part of the cultural landscape.

www.ingramcontent.com/pod-product-compliance
Lightning Source LLC
Chambersburg PA
CBHW061445160726
47995CB00003B/1042